NATIONAL
GEOGRAPHIC

From the Skyscraper

Marvin Buckley

From the skyscraper
I can see streets.

People drive on the streets.

5

From the skyscraper
I can see office buildings.

**People work in
the office buildings.**

8

From the skyscraper
I can see a park.

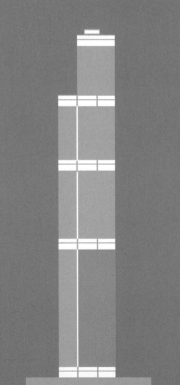

11

People jog in the park.

From the skyscraper
I can see a lake.

**People sail boats
on the lake.**

16

17

From the skyscraper
I can see an airport.

19

People get on planes
at the airport.

From the skyscraper
I can see a baseball field.

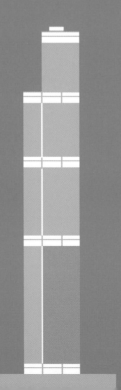

People enjoy the big game.